Our Lives With COPD The Truth

Our Lives With COPD The Truth

MJP Padre

Copyright © 2022 by MJP Padre.

ISBN:	Softcover	978-1-6698-2609-5
	eBook	978-1-6698-2610-1

All rights reserved. No part of this book may be reproduced or transmitted in any form or by any means, electronic or mechanical, including photocopying, recording, or by any information storage and retrieval system, without permission in writing from the copyright owner.

This is a work of fiction. Names, characters, places and incidents either are the product of the author's imagination or are used fictitiously, and any resemblance to any actual persons, living or dead, events, or locales is entirely coincidental.

Any people depicted in stock imagery provided by Getty Images are models, and such images are being used for illustrative purposes only.
Certain stock imagery © Getty Images.

Print information available on the last page.

Rev. date: 05/19/2022

To order additional copies of this book, contact:
Xlibris
844-714-8691
www.Xlibris.com
Orders@Xlibris.com
843115

Dedicated to those of us on the long hard road we walk around the globe and to our family, friends and caregivers who walk this road with us.

The people in this book are between the ages of 50 to 81 years old. They grew up in the world when smoking was encouraged and glamorized. The commercials of the Marlboro Man on his horse in a ranch hands clothes in a Ranch corral leaning against a fence…this was when the commercials on the TV were selling cigarettes….the magazines were full of ads and you could light up with your doctor in his or her office. This was the era where the commercial of the man smoking a pipe showed him as an intellectual or the man with the cigar was a Man's Man. This was the age when movies and TV were glamorizing smoking where certain characters were known by their cigarette or pipe or cigar. Some of us never smoked, we got the disease from 2nd. hand smoke, bad air quality, factory dust and the sorts.

This book is about the lives of countless numbers of COPD sufferers around the world. In it you will find personal comments about various subjects of the disease and how it affects us in our lives and our wishes and our losses. Please read this in order to gather knowledge of what your loved one, friend or patient is really going through and how you may in a small or large way can understand us and help us. This book is being written in 2022 to give you a time frame for some of the answers to the questions.

MJP Padre

A special thank you to the Staff of Stuff That Works, thank you for putting together this international community because without you and your offering this book would not exist.

My eternal thanks to the following for graciously offering comments for the book. We would not have this without all of you. I am blessed to know you.

MJP Padre

Peter England	Steve 2936
Sandy USA	Veronica 1023
Dave 2341	Pam 2731
Karen 9485	Anonymous 76753
Tina 765	Doug 293
Pamela 627	Julia 941
Tom 1980	Julie 1782
Steve 2930	Michele 131
Monica 1409	Mindy 426
Angela 6103	Susan 1248
Elaine 2601	Diane 1212
Raewyn 79	Stanys
Bill 100	Valerie 2299
Jill 2262	Kathy 3928

Pamela

Michael

Christine 5780

Joe 306

Iva 15

Jody 623

Suzanne 1111

Kay 1864

Shelley 1160

Don 838

Linda 9038

Alfreda 26

Shanna 9

Avie, Scotland

Thomas 31

Audrey 1146

Pamela 627

Alana 350

Rose 1695

627 Karl 148

Dek 62

Mary 8215

Monica 1409

Kat 123

David 2212

Denise 3439

Jeane 10

Robert 3603

Pam 2118

Valerie 1915

Mark 1583

Martin 1179

Judy 2806

Karen 10174

Gail 1998

Karl 178

Jim, Canada

Linda 7046

Janet 2341	Jim 1750
James 371	Mike 3012
Graham 722	Judy 1726
June 205	Lynne 1688
Jeannine 41	Terry 1543
Anonymous 74422	Pam 2668
Alfred 26	Frank 381
Marlin	Jane 4863
Anonymous 116244	Jack 1221
Caryn 78	Genevieve 201
Barbara 1430	Brenda 4130
Brenda 1774	Bree 29413
Derek 309	Susan 1248
Pamela 2273	Ronnie 268
Janice 2030	Elaine 2601
Howard 30	Janice 1136
Antony 92	Sue 6257
Cynthia 1429	Christine 5152
Bill 1400	Char 43652

Valerie 2299

Thomas 31

Becky MI

Anonymous 59398

Josie 797

Mindy 426

Tom – Hardy

Jim 1702

Banjo Alan

Douglas 263

Paul 4379

Penny 1217

Stephen 2260

Donna 2309

Shirley 287

Tom 1056

Maureen 1898

Alan 493

Jen 2316

Judy 2806

Karen 10174

Michelle 131

Monica 409

Laurie Lynn

Ronnie

Suzanne 361

Mary 4858

David 6261

Barbara 4458

Cathy 225

Stella 455

User 66380

Judy 2940

Alan 1548

Natty 24

Glenice 2

Jo 2884

George 51

David 6037

Donna 43

Anonymous 49025

Way 582

Maureen 1898

Pam 2118

Carol 5242

Kelly 2622

Linda 4086

Marie 3325

Robert 2941

Carol 5254

Jean 2110

Richard 767

Anonymous 65295

Barbara 4130

Carol 5254

Sharon 5910

Roxanne 454

User 20524

Tina 1339

Marcia 494

Barbara 1430

Shirley287

Helen

Janice

Sue5679

Donna 2309

Bradley 47

Terry 855

Michael 4314

Miracle 21

Helen 788

Dianne 719

Patricia 4754

Bernie 113

John 4119

Dianne 2286

Sue 6409

Richard 2044

Luis 28

Stan 13

Brenda 876

Nan 1011

Nancy 3281

Patti 59

Martin 1197

Judy 1676

Donna 5667

Cindy 1275

Harry 321

Cary112

Debbra 13

Vikkie 4

Dawn – 53

Tyler 21

Anonymous 95266

Nancy 3281

Leanne 1307

Judi 279

CONTENTS

Chapter 1 What Caused Your COPD? 1

Chapter 2 How Has Your Life Changed With COPD? ... 13

Chapter 3 What Do You Do when Having A Bad Day? 29

Chapter 4 Exercise 34

Chapter 5 What Would You Tell A Young Person
About Smoking? 42

Chapter 6 Help From Family and Friends? 45

Chapter 7 How Is Your Medical Care? 58

Chapter 8 How Friends and Family Can Help Best? 76

Chapter 1

The question I have asked first Concerns with how ones COPD is caused. I have asked the folks what their COPD was caused from and what stage they are. Some countries and doctors do not tell patients what their stage is and some people do not want to know. Most people think COPD is caused by smoking. This is not always the case as you will see here in the following answers.

"My COPD was caused by Vietnam, dusty work place, years of smoking and ignoring indicators. Diagnosed in 2000 and have been told I have end stage COPD."

"I was diagnosed 15 years ago mainly caused by years of smoking a pack a day. Not sure what stage I am at and really do not want to know."

"I was diagnosed 40 years ago, smoking, Industrial processes and asbestos. No idea what stage."

"Never smoked in my life but COPD may be from other people's smoke. My colleagues at work, very smokey in pubs. Plus and asthmatic childhood."

"Hi Steve, only diagnosed April 23rd. 2021…..mine is partly caused from smoking but I also have something called Neurofibromatosis related lung disease which causes fibromas and cysts on the lung. It is a very rare lung condition and adds severe COPD emphysema and my lungs are deteriorating quite rapidly because I have gone from 3 liters of oxygen to 9 liters in less than a year and my gut tells me I'm going to 10 liters at my chest clinic apt. in 2 weeks. I don't like those stage brackets because it can add extra stress and anxiety to ones' condition and my doctor's do not use them either. I only know it is severe because it is on my discharge letter. I also believe I had some kind of an allergic reaction to the jab (covid shot) because this time last year there was no mention of COPD in my life, I even had an operation 6 months prior to my diagnosis and no mention of it. It was while I was in the hospital for the 2nd. Operation that it kicked off very quickly within my 4 weeks of having my first one."

"Hi Steve, 2006 lung cancer stage 3, removal of right upper lung. Emphysema and COPD diagnosis after chemo."

"Smoking for many years as a hairdresser, for many years hair spray, acrylics for nails. Diagnosed 2019 but sure I had it before then just ignored the signs."

"Didn't get diagnosed with Pulminary Sarcoidosis until 2012. Chest X-rays showed nodules which led to VATS surgery. Have been in the care of a Pulmonologist since. I don't cough nor have phlem fortunately. Doctor wanted me to go for lung transplant evaluation but after reading their 172 page booklet I know that I am not a candidate at this time. Will be discussing this with my Pulmonary doctor this month."

"Steve, Since I smoked, I assume that caused the COPD. I was diagnosed at age 58 and am just about 72. I don't know what stage I am at and do not want to know."

"Smoking pipe for the last 35 years. Stage 4 for the past 3 years."

"They say smoking caused the COPD. I'M END STAGE AND HAVE HAD IT 17 YEARS."

"Asthma and smoking and environmental. Here in the UK they don't have to tell you what stage you're at. Was diagnosed 15 years ago."

"Mine was smoking and ignoring the signs of it earlier in the piece as I listened to the wheeze even as I smoked. Don't know what stage. Mine was complicated by another lung disease called Interstitial lung disease or ILD which I got 7 years ago from another disease I have called Lupus. In theory I have got the COPD on the inside and have the ILD on the outside and interesting though as the ILD has stopped progressing."

"Caused mainly by smoking, I'd say I am moderate stage plus. Diagnosed 2014."

"Caused by dust and mold from farming and cigarettes. Diagnosed 10 years ago at 25% lung capacity but have had it much longer than that to a lesser degree."

"Smoking caused mine for sure, was diagnosed 10 years ago but am sure I had around 15 years."

"I am 71 years old and have smoked since I was 13 I suppose. The doctors have told me always to give the smokes away but since then I have had open heart surgery (aortic valve replacement) but still going strong. Have been diagnosed with severe emphysema and COPD but still enjoy riding my motor bike and boating."

"Smoking is the main cause. Don't know what stage. Bad cause I use oxygen at night when exerting myself. I've had it since 1985 (40 years) diagnosed in 2014."

"Smoking caused mine, diagnosed 16 years ago, only bothered me the last 6. Don't want to know what stage I am. Day 96 without a cigarette (Yes I am counting the days).- Authors note – 4/6/22 is the date of the note."

"Smoking caused my COPD. I was diagnosed 22 years ago and am at stage 3."

"Cause – smoking / chemical dust. Stage 4, had it for 6 years it could have bern longer. Started getting short of breath in 1988."

"A PACK A Day FOR 67 YEARS. I don't know what stage but it must be getting near the end."

"I am an ex-smoker and was diagnosed just over 2 years ago. I do not know what stage I'm at (not told) and am not on oxygen. I am 71 years old and live in Australia."

"Diagnosed stage 2, 8 months ago, I was not a smoker but was married to a heavy smoker 40 years ago. Dr. said I was smoking right along with him (Second hand smoke did damage)."

"Hi Steve, My COPD caused by smoking. Diagnosed 9 years ago. Don't know what stage I'm at."

"I have had it for 16 years, caused from smoking and working without a mask in a dusty environment plus I had prostate cancer and the radiation really slowed my immune system down. Now using inhalers and nebuli- sers at night, I have an air machine because I stop breathing when sleeping. You have to make the best of it."

"Stage 4- not on oxygen yet. Had it 12 years. "(From smoking)."

"Hey Steve, I was only diagnosed a few months ago…..mild COPD is what I have…..for me it is smoking."

"Had a bad cold in 2014 with a ruff cough, discovered I was getting breathless going upstairs. Was sent to practice nurse who did a Spiro check on me then said I had COPD. I was at that time 32% lung capacity!! I got over cold and was put on Spriva (which I could not get on with) appeared fine until September 2018 which I ended up in the hospital with Pneumonia. At that time was really busy with work trying to get everything covered up and documented to handover to new field supervisor as I was retiring. Was going out at 6am and coming home at 9pm to carry on working on working. So I really did myself damage!!! Not that it was really appreciated!!! So retired 9th. August 2018. In hospital 5th. September in very poor state!!!! That is where I learnt by reading my discharge papers I was a carbon dioxide retainer. I also really was almost informed that I had emphysema but was not really as a remark from doctor at hospital to students around my bed!!!. Was never explained to me and still hasn't been!!!. Came out after 6 days unable to walk far as hadn't been out of bed so legs were weak. Have had so much experience with hospitals not really encouraging people out of bed to walk!!!. It makes me mad!!!. Anyway was moved to Trimbo which suits me fine and finally Ventolin inhaler which I had been asking for after my surgery for 3 years. Haven't seen a COPD Doctor for 2 years and a half, but do have a great respiratory team that I fully trust!! They appear to have the time to sit and explain."

"I was a smoker from age 20 to 61 at least 20 to 30 a day. I also worked for a few years in a factory with powder resin and hot ovens making little sinks for dentists, this was all undertaken without ventilation or face coverings. so maybe that did not help!! Along with me wanting everything super clean I used ammonia and have to admit a few times had myself gasping for air. So really apart from adverts. and films depicting smoking as a glamorous thing I have done myself awful damage. I'm slow at what I do but still alive to be with the ones I love."

"Still think COPD should be highlighted more as people really need to be aware!!!.

Sorry for the long worded comments. Good luck with your venture things need to be put out there.

Also ordinary people need to know what help they can be. I suspect stage 4 due to last lung test 27% in 2019. Haven't been told and really don't want to know as it will give me more stress."

"Diagnosed about 2015 at that time quit smoking. Not sure what stage I'm at."

"Probably caused by smoking. Diagnosed a year ago but probably had for several years. Never been given a stage and don't want to know."

"Asbestos, cigarettes and bronchitis since a child. Stage 4. Diagnosed over 24 years ago."

"The doctors have never been able to figure it why I have COPD, since I've never smoked. They just shake their heads.

My theory is that I was exposed to second – hand smoke from birth. My father smoked a pipe. That was part of his identity. When I was about 10 I asked him if it was ok to smoke a pipe, since cigarettes were harmful. He said no, because a pipe smoker's don't inhale. Neither of us thought about second – hand smoke – I don't think at the time the term had even been invented. I was exposed to that smoke until I left home at 20. In addition, my father took pride in building roaring fires in the fireplace, and we had those fires going most nights throughout the winter. Walking into the house, you could smell the smoke. Wood – smoke it smelled good, but it was also a lot of particular matter circulating in the room. You'd go outside and the smoke from the chimney would spread around the whole neighborhood.

So I think it was all that smoke for 20 years, plus work in the 70's at least half the office workers where I worked smoked and I'm sure it did not help.

There are a couple houses about 3 blocks away from where I live right now who use their fireplaces quite frequently during the winter. They don't need them for heat because the houses were built in the 60's and early 70's, but it is obviously important that they have their fires. They both have firewood stacked neatly at the sides of their houses, running the whole width of their houses. I used to groan every time I drove past because I knew that wood was going to end up smoke. Now I just look the other way when I go by. When they have a fire going, the smoke often drifts all the way to where we are. If it's that bad, I have to go back inside."

Chapter 2

The following question I have asked folks is "how has their life changed." Our lives have changed. For some of us there have not been too many changes yet for others dramatically. There are some of us because of just COPD and others with a combination of covid and other things also.

"My life is much more restricted and I am fatigued more.".

"It hasn't restricted my life too much at this point. It is harder to do with ease and I had to give up the Boston Marathon(LOL!), but I know things will change."

"I go out less because of the logistics of the oxygen and planning how long I can be away before the oxygen runs out. Also fatigued which doesn't help."

"Going out doesn't happen that much anymore because have time waver around O2 cylinder. Takes so much longer to do the smallest tasks and I am getting slower at it!! Fatigue is another factor. My brain doesn't function as well as it used to – thankfully my husband is patient and can understand my gibberish."

"My life had done a complete 180 since COPD. Obviously never smoke a cigarette or Marijuana, cigars etc…My grandfather died at 100 and he never smoked in his life."

"I have been short tempered and irritable and angry that I can't jog, play tennis or golf."

"7 years ago when I was diagnosed it was after a trip that I had saved to go on and got very sick on the cruise. My life began to change when I got out of the hospital the first time and changed more and more each time after the next 5 times I was admitted. I was very careful about being around people and it was when I was diagnosed at 75% and covid hit that I quit things. In Sacramento, Ca in the USA I had put together a program for helping Homeless Veterans where I had gathered a group of people and we gathered food and clothing and I opened up a small 2 bookcase library at the local vet. center. I had to quit this and shut the program down. I had to quit my American Legion meetings as I could not be around people as well as other activities. 12 weeks ago I was told I am at 50% and have less things I do. I have had time to write 3 novels and am currently writing a 4th. Civil War novel and am also writing this book. We had planned to travel but that is out. I have told my wife to live her life as she has a very active social life as she is a volunteer at the local zoo and has been for over 28 years and goes out to lunch, breakfast and dinner with ladies she used to work with as they are all retired. Yes, I am angry at this though as it has altered my life but that is just the way it is and I have to accept it. I do not shop other than just when the store opens and I only shop if my wife cannot get it for me. I have been out shopping maybe 6 times since covid started. We started going out to lunch a couple of months ago. We get to the place right as they open there and we get a table way away from anyone else and we eat fast. Then for the next 5 to 7 days I panic as I pray I have not been exposed to covid. Since I was diagnosed I have done very few holidays with the family. Only Easter twice as they were outside. I have not been to Christmas in 7 years as I have young Great Nephews and they always have colds and I cannot catch a cold. In addition to this I have severe back problems that also cause me problems. It is especially hard as I can only sit at the computer for a couple of hours at a time and then I have to take a day off before I can get back onto the computer. This makes it hard to write any of my books." (Note…as of 5/12/22 I now have a Handi-capped parking plackard for my car and when shopping in stores I have to ride one of the electric scooters as I lose my breath when walking around the stores). MJP Padre

"I hardly go anywhere since covid started and sadly it is still rampant in Ireland."

"I have received the Moderna vaccine and booster. I watch the local risk levels and am careful with masking and separation but I go out. Life always has some risk."

"interested and grateful when they read our stories."

"Yes I have had all the shots and due to back issues I pretty much can't go out. I feel like I'm on lockdown all the time, and now they are saying a new virus has started up. "Someone" is really mad at us and how we have treated the earth."

"It took me 12 months to come to terms with my condition before I resigned from my job."

"Hi Steve, Yes, life has changed a lot. I have given up many things, not just because of COPD but also because of the danger of catching covid with COPD. We learn to dance on a moving carpet and do what we can."

"Yes I have had to give up golf and dog obedience but still have reading and good friends -. Tis annoying."

"We've been out of lockdown since early December and I've decided to get on with life. Two years out of what I have left is ENOUGH. I've been lunching all week with friends once a week, going to Chinese once a week with a group that have had to take an extended break and even been shopping a couple of times. Coffee with friends at the beach and grandchildren in the holidays. It's nearly back to normal (just been washing my hands and avoiding crowds)."

"Hi Steve, my life has changed in so many ways since COPD and covid. I am 81 years old and have had COPD since 2010. Been home bound for the last couple of years. I was always an active person, not necessarily exercise, but I loved to go shopping and belonged to a volunteer club….we played bingo with nursing Home residents, collected clothing and hygiene products and gave them to the homeless. We had fundraisers, made bags with blankets and toys for the children taken out of their homes when parents were arrested and many more services for our communities.

Now I feel so useless. Can barely take care of myself. I have to have my children help me with the Dr. appts. and I go out to eat with friends once a week. Even those things are very hard to do. Just to bathe and dress is a major task being so breathless. Last year they discovered a mass in my lower left lung and could not operate because of my lungs so they did radiation. Going for another scan next month to see if it is stable. Then I found out I have pulmonary hypertension and when I was hospitalized in December they did an echogram and said I had congestive heart failure. I have family that is so helpful I don't know what I would do without them but I miss being able to play with my great grandchildren. I miss that I can't get down and play like we used to. Thanks for letting me vent."

"Hi Steve, I live several states away from my family. Since covid I have not risked visiting or returned to my normal lifestyle. It's frustrating but with chronic Emphysema my health professional advise me to be patient."

"Steve, covid did not stop my family from normal living. Yet COPD did for me. My family are smokers and I cannot be around them. I had to stop seeing them to live. I have gotten so lonely that I asked my son to come and get me. I have had just my own company since Christmas. I have to chance being around people. Loneliness sucks."

"Hi Steve, Yes I have had to give up a lot of things. Not only do I have COPD I have PAU, but I have a chronic back pain which is getting worse. I have been very careful about going out and have my groceries, meds. and dog food delivered. My back keeps me from doing anything."

"Absolutely Steve, used to walk up the highest peaks. Now it is just around the reservoirs. Looking up at the peaks makes me cry. Also used to love Tai Chi not to bad found qi gong, similar but more gentle also cycling. Looking around for an e-bike I can actually afford. Sure pal, it's a pain but there's always an alternative once you get your head around it. Good Luck Mate."

"Steve, UK – many changes have had to be made as I can't manage so much. I need now to get back to exercising to build my fitness as I feel exhausted all the time."

"Hi Steve, I have been writing my memoirs. I have been adding to them for several years now. But now I found when I can't sleep at night it is a wonderful distraction to get up and type a few paragraphs. It takes my mind off of breathlesness too. I think further generations will be interested when they read our stories."

"Hi Steve, many of my charity groups took a hiatis for 2 years- not meeting in public. They are meeting now. My birthday club just started back up once a month dinners. My century club is back and meeting once a month for the last 7 months. My husband and I are traveling right now spending 3 months in Central America. I try to stay as active as I can with lots of walking, short hikes and craft projects as I can. I'm stage 3 but I push on as much as I can. There is so much traveling I want to do. It's frustrating when I cannot hike up a mountain but I do something else – walk on the beach – I'm grateful for each day. Just keep moving and stay positive."

"My life has changed to. 1. After having covid a year past January, 2. Then going through the long covid, 3. And to be told you have mild COPD…..has been a very hard time for me. I was always on the go, did everything without effort even on my bike but haven't been on that since this year. Stopped smoking 9 years ago…now so tired, breathless, tired and sore…..but I'm still here and getting on with it."

"Yes, my life has been hampered and the reality is that probably within the next year I'm going to have to give up farming and am not too sure now how I will emotionally deal with it. I guess I will have find out!! My hospital gave me a CD of all my X-rays and scans on request when I told them what for – I've a right to them anyway. I know at least 3 people I stopped from smoking and not all of them were teenagers either. I make no secret of the fact that I have COPD so when I lean against the cattle yards getting my breath they know what it is from."

"My life has been greatly disrupted, my thoracic surgeon believed I needed to smell the roses 16 years on, my life is now very slow, many attempts are required to do small tasks."

"My life has been changed drastically. I can no longer walk or do any of my usual activities. I have had to have a disabled shower fitted and I also use a mobility scooter to get out and about. I'm still determined to do as much as I can and am travelling to Spain next week to visit my daughter….hopefully the weather is good and I can get out every day because here in Glasgow I don't get out much."

From a partner's Point of view……."We have to plan every outing. Sometimes we can't go at all. My partner says that he feels he has to make the most of his time just taking care of his health. He feels like that is not how he planned on living the rest of his life. Sometimes he just doesn't feel like doing the work that contributes to improving your health, he just gets tired….and he really has a good positive attitude. He wants to drive across country from Oregon to Illinois in the near future. A year ago we could do this without much planning. Now every day is to try the things he is learning in pulmonary therapy so that he can gauge whether we will be able to make this trip or not. He is experiencing some improvement, two months ago this trip would have been out of the question I didn't think he would be able to walk into the hotel room from the car to spend the night. But now I'm pretty confident he will be able to do it."

"I was a carer and used to walk a lot to all my jobs no problems, now I struggle walking across the road to my neighbors' house."

"It's starting to affect me, I'm slowing down and tire easily."

"Once I was a very independent person. COPD has made me rely on others for assistance or even the simplest tasks. I struggle with everything from housework to food shopping.

However my husband is an amazing support and cares for me quite well and does so without making me feel less than."

"I am not as active as I used to be, need a lot of rest."

"I have to think before going anywhere. If I am walking will there be hills? Will my coughing disturb people?"

"My life has gone downhill since being diagnosed with COPD. I used to love to dance can't do that anymore, liked long hikes now only…..with a walker, liked to shop now it's a chore, don't go out because of covid don't go because it attacks the lungs, going upstairs is a chore. The price of cigarettes here in Canada are 18.00 dollars a package…wow. I try to do the best I can because I brought this on myself. Getting thru a day is a chore some days are worse than others but I carry on. I try to stay positive for the most part, I can do that. It was 1961 when I started smoking and at that time everyone was, my Mom, Dad, Brother all my friends, you could go to the doctor and sit in his office and have a smoke with him, you could smoke in bars, restaurants, bingo halls even hospitals being a patient and of course once you're hooked your doomed. It would be so nice if cigarettes were banned but why would the government do that, their making far too much money of the taxes. I could go on but I'm sure I've said enough. Thanks for hearing me out. Enjoy the day everyone. Hugs from Canada."

"I don't feel like doing all the things I used to like walking the mall, having sex (Good thing I do not have a partner right now, Haha) doing housework is difficult right now. I don't feel like cooking very much at all. I don't travel now at all with covid out there."

"often tired, can't walk as much as I used to. I have to stop for a couple of minutes rest on my way."

"Most things I do are much harder to do with COPD. I have to take breaks mopping the floor or vacuuming. I don't go up 2 flights of stairs at once. I need to stop in between. I can't keep up with my Grandkids anymore."

"COPD made it impossible to keep up with my healthy friends. I was and am limited to where I can go. Fumes of any kind cause coughing fits and have to use an inhaler. Smokers in my family didn't understand what is it is like for me trying to be around them which isolates me, I went 4 months alone now I have made up my mind to live around my family of smokers. Better than isolation."

"Activities are restricted."

"Yes, I got a new car in 2018 and now it has 3200 miles on it. I do grocery shopping and the pharmacy is the place I go to the most. I love being a hermit!!!."

"My bowling league disbanded and our alley got sold. It's now a Tractor Supply Store. I do miss bowling. I also quit going to the store and out to dinner. No exercise for 2 years and now struggling to walk across the room without losing my breath!! Just started going to the hair dresser." …..Authors note: Keep on exercising to the best of your ability with this disease!!!. With your doctors guidance.

"Hi Steve, this time last year I was still working full time as a primary cook, a Mum to a 17 year old and 20 year old sons and also a hands on Grandma to my 3 year old grandson every weekend while his Mum went to work. But I was becoming more and more short of breath until I found out in May that I have severe COPD. After lung function tests which came Back at 23%, CT scans etc..for my diagnosis I now spend my days at home struggling to ds the slightest of things that involve moving around and can say my life has changed dramatically."

"Since being diagnosed with COPD five years ago, I have had to quit most of my outdoor activities: hiking, kayaking, cycling, I used to work out regularly: now I still workout, bit only do one set instead of three, with much reduced weights. I don't do any travelling – chronic fatigue has really slowed me down.

Chapter 3

Question – When you are having a bad day like all of us who suffer from this disease what do you do to bring up your spirits?

"I listen to music and read and enjoy my cat sitting on my lap as she brings me peace and joy. I go and work on various hobbies I can still do with the disease and my bad back. I am also a recovering alcoholic and I can get onto Zoom and attend meetings and this really helps. In addition on the computer I have found speakers on AA subjects who are very funny and it gets me laughing. I am a writer and work on the books about civil war units my relatives fought with. It requires a lot of research and it takes my mind off my disease.

I recommend that people write about their lives for future generations. There is nothing worse than trying to write a book about someone 4 generations before and have nothing much about them. I am also able to talk with my wife and she listens and comments for me."

"I take it easy, go to bed, sleep, go on the computer to watch Ted Talks on you tube……nothing like a bit of learning to give you something else to think about besides yourself. Read a book, pick a flower, write your memoirs."

"Hi Steve. In all honesty I listen to Absolute 80's all day Monday to Friday until 5pm then it's TV time, Netflix or Football and I do not watch news anymore. I was only diagnosed last April and as I think you already know I'm also living with chronic pain since October 2019. I visited some pretty dark places but I put myself in therapy last year as well as anti-depressants. For the past 5 or 6 months I've managed to keep myself positive most day's and this community (as well as being in 6 others) helps me so much, it's like a second family to me(even though most of my family are pretty useless except my daughter) and I think I have a lot of empathy towards others. The COPD and Clinical Depression Communities keep me on my toes especially this one, LOL. I don't get many low points and normally only last 2 or 3 day's (although I was struggling a few weeks ago what with elbow, nightmares, struggling with breathlessness so it went on for about a week) but when I do the people in this community get me through it or I just come on, stay in bed, don't eat and I've been known to take a sleeping tablet in the afternoon, wake up in the evening take my nighttime meds. And go back to sleep again (I still wake up several times though) it's naughty taking a tablet in the afternoon but I just want to shut the world out because that's the only thing that helps me then I normally just wake up in the morning after a few days and I am fine again. Sorry for the length."

"I do Yoga everyday with Meditation, I garden, swim, dance walk my dogs. I have an excellent Pulmonary team which I can ring with any concerns, a physio therapist and a GP all extremely good bonds. I also have a woman's group I Have attended for 15 years and we dance each week, Wu Tao. It now contains sound healing PIES – Physical, Intellectual, Emotional, Spiritual. We check in with these emotions, say what we are feeling, check out. Once an emotion is verbalized it loses power."

"Tiktok, Instagram or just stay still and listen to my body and when I fee out of sorts go for a walk on the Bush cross the road, go to the beach, burn some essential oils to cheer me up, be thankful for all the time I have left in my life, sometimes ring my Mum, she is 96, still very with it, we have a bet going, I will out - live her, this is always up lifting even though I don't own up to feeling like crap. LOL!."

"Concentrate on my breathing and try not to over think things and just rest."

"Illness is very disruptive in your body, causing chaos in the affected systems. When I am down or fatigued, I fight back as much as I can, even in very small ways, by bringing some sense of order too my external environment. On a very bad day, that can be as small as cleaning my glasses with soap in soap and warm water, to get them really clean, or cleaning up my in-box, or sorting and filling the pile of papers on my desk. Although these are small things, it gives me a sense of accomplishment to have put a corner of my world in order, and with one small thing accomplished, I may choose to go on to another small thing, and gradually through the morning or the day, put more and more of my world in order and start to feel I am at least counterbalancing some of the chaos occurring inside of me."

Chapter 4

We are all at different stages of this disease. Depending on what stage you are and what you are able to do, what do you do for exercise? …Authors note…before starting any exercise program check with your doctor!!.

"I use Air Physio I got on line and it helps."

"I'm finding it hard to walk across the room. On Oxygen 24/7 and sinuses are inflamed so not getting needed oxygen. Have tried several nasal sprays nothing works. I'm doing chair pulmonary exercises on You Tube. I am hoping these will build up my breathing so I will be able to walk further."

"Lung Specialist said I'm at 65%, weather permitting I walk each morning with 1kg weight on each limb-work in my garden for 1 – 2 hours per day – seeing heart specialist as it has issues, will let you know if there are any improvement as both cause fatigue."

"I also use Air physio, water and weed our large garden and potted plants, do some exercises to music though nothing too much, lift tins of baked beans(I don't have weights), walk around my unit and into appointments, but often can't walk due to gout."

"I've been given an exercise plan but don't do them. I am my own worst enemy."

"Qi gong – Look up Lee Holden, he has some great routines."

"Lung function 15%, peddles, balancing disc, wall pushups to stretch for upper body."

"Hi Steve, I am at stage 4 have had COPD for over 30 years. Right now I use anywhere between 2 to 4 liters of Oxygen. I can walk 3 to 4 miles I am helping to rebuild a house doing carpentry work, I use better breathing exercises I learned in Pulmonary Rehabilitation, the main thing is to keep moving as much as possible when you have this disease."

"I have COPD but not to the stage where I am badly incapacitated and find that swimming and pool walking are good for lung exercises."

"A little bit of gardening but that is about all."

"I still drive a vehicle, do my own shopping and have back stairs when hanging washing. Fortunately I'm not on Oxygen just Ventol and Spillito puffers and I have gotten an Air Physio which I seldom use."

"Stage 4, FEV1-28% for last 3 years. Walk on treadmill for 30 minutes to an hour with short (3 min.) breaks to do back bends every 15 minutes. Some light weight strength exercises every other day. This is all done in air conditioning and under a ceiling fan. It has taken some time to work up to this but I really think this has helped slow down the progress."

"I do have a gym pass and aim to use it twice a week. Still am able to carry out housework with not too much trouble and I attend chair yoga once a week. Even managed to mow my front nature-strip this week which took some effort but I got it done."

"I try to hike 4 miles at a minimum of 4 times weekly."

"I'm on 5ltrs of oxygen but still try and do weights workout every couple of days just got to take my time and have 2 minute intervals between reps."

"6 minute or step ups on bottom step 3x10 I walk on spots most days and have small weights which I lift above my head and to my side 3x10. I try and do this every day not all at once just spread it over the morning as that's the best time. I do use my portable oxygen. Not saying this is easy!!! In fact sometimes I think why do I bother!!. But I'm still here!!!."

"I have 50% lung capacity and going to the gym 3 days a week with a trainer. I find this is better than walking."

"Right now I think I'm most likely stage 4 not that I have been told or want to know!!!. But the OAST flo test I did was 27% that was 3 years ago!!!. I try and walk in my house or garden for 10 minutes very slowly. I have a small cycle exercise machine which I use daily for 6 minutes. I walk up and down my stairs for 6 minutes or step ups on bottom step 3x10."

"Hi Steve, I caught TB when I was working at a hospital in an area with high TB incidence. I was smoking then, and had difficulty stopping, but registrar at the TB clinic bawled me out so effectively that I quit because I couldn't face him telling me that I had a child to think of.!!!. But I was living in an area with high traffic pollution, and slowly my symptoms got worse and I developed COPD, but with Spuriva and Sirdupla and Ventolin I can walk miles and swim 4 or 5 days a week, usually 40 lengths of the pool. (I am 77 now), I know that if

I hadn't quit smoking I would have died a few years ago. The tobacco firms don't care if you die, we are nothing to them."

"I try and do exercise tapes 6 days a week for 3 miles – the last mile I am struggling for sure but I just started doing the 3 miles. My knees on down get very painful so that slows me up for sure but I try to keep moving some anyway. During the Spring, Summer and Fall I try and spend as much time outside as I can working in the flowers bed and garden."

"I'm doing chair pulmonary exercises on You Tube. I'm hoping these will build up breathing."

"I don't know what stage I am at and don't want to know. For exercise I walk my dog a mile or two a day and I do dance workout for Senior's by following a video from You Tube. I also do all of my own housework and have been doing all my own yard work."

"I go to the gym 3 days per week and lift light weights on weight machines. I find that this works best as it just works certain muscle groups at a time and supports all the other muscles. This really works my lungs a great deal and I have found that his has really improved my breathing. My lungs get a real good workout as I am breathing very heavily during my workout. There is an indoor heated pool at my club and once the weather warms up in the morning once Spring really gets here I will be going back to the pool and walking laps to help my lower back 2 days per week. I suffer from Disintegrating discs all through my spine, 5 lumbar have scoliosis and I have arthritis all through my spine. This causes me all kinds of problems. But with the exercises things go along pretty well. I just have to stay on it. They say, use it or lose it. (5/12/22 I have recently had to lessen my weights a lot as I have been exhausted to the point of having trouble breathing and moving about too much for about 3 hours after a workout, if it does not improve I will go to walking laps in a pool." MJP Padre)

"There is a Chinese saying, so I am told, that the legs go first, Therefore, I try to walk an hour a day, if the weather is cool, or if it is raining, or windy, I stay in and walk on my treadmill. I bought a basic one because I can't walk on any kind of an incline, so don't need that (expensive) feature. I just do what I can do. I set the speed to 2.1 miles per hour. I tried 2.1 miles per hour and that just wiped me out. So 2.1 is my baseline. With COPD the urge is very strong to just sit around and watch TV all day. I have a series of exercises I do on a rotating basis, glutes, upper body, and legs, and don't forget the Abs!!. You Tune has literally hundreds of exercises for older people. I also do exercises to loosen up, hip flexors because with all the sitting we do, they tend to get tighter. In fact, standing in general is good. I can feel the results all day after going through a stretching exercise sequence."

Chapter 5

Question. What would you tell a young person who has just taken up smoking?

"As for young people, there is no point in telling them not to smoke. I try to explain to them the impact it has had on me and hope that sinks in somewhere along the road."

"Don't start, it takes away your independence and you have to think about everything you want to do and plan carefully, even for a walk."

"Same thing my Mom told me that I did not listen to PLZ don't smoke, it will kill you!!! Or make your life horrific."

"My son asked me the other day while I was driving him home from work" I was thinking of getting a vape stick... What do you think?" I stopped the car in the middle of the road and got a hold of him and told him in no uncertain terms that if he wanted to end up like me then go ahead. I opened up his door, told him to get out and walk home while he still could.!!!"

"I would definitely tell a teen not to smoke – but I doubt they'd listen to anyone any more than I did."

"It has been said by others, teens think they are immortal. I'm saying that I'd ask them to volunteer in a hospice - the realities of life and death- Good and Bad choices - it's up to the individual to make those choices and to live with the consequences however painful they may be."

"I would tell them they are on the slippery slope to serious health issues and to look at the state in it."

"These days there is more evidence and knowledge that young people have access to regarding the damage smoking does however I would tell them" don't do it "unless they wanted to end up like me or worse."

"I of course would strongly discourage a teenager from taking up smoking, but what might make a greater impression is to have them read these posts."

"I wouldn't tell a teenager not to smoke, normally the young don't like being told being preached to, furthermore most are immortal most young healthy youngsters never think of what damage smoking can do. Some will tell you they can stop smoking any time they wish. I know this from past experience warning youngsters."

Chapter 6

We all have needs and some of us more than others. In what ways do you your friends and family members help you that you really appreciate.

"They help me with heavy things as I get winded with trying to lift things. They carry things for me a distance of any kind. I am really bad at asking for help. After 2 months of not asking for help to move something in the garage I asked my wife to move a couple of boxes in the garage. She was very happy to help and it was very easy to do for her. There was no way I could have done it. I asked her to do this because I had a project I had put off because I could not move the boxes. I was able to move the boxes initially as I was pulling them and it took time but could not push them back in place. She was a life saver and I got my project done that afternoon. I told her I owe her lunch. She tells me not to fast and get winded and walks slowly so I will slow sown. She does all my driving as my back is getting to bad as well as I am to winded from shopping to drive. She takes care of the house and does all the shopping and cooking. We have gardeners who come in every Saturday. I make my own lunch and breakfast if any and she makes my morning coffee. She takes great care of me and I am very blessed. I absolutely do not know what I would do without her." MJP Padre

"I have a former partner who comes and helps with the composting. Cleaning the bathroom and washing floors and changing the linen."

"My husband does all the cooking, washing and ironing."

"This definitely does not happen except the washing, he has anxiety issues after a stroke so needs to do things in a routine always making me cups of tea but never has cooked or cleaned. But adding to this my daughter helps so much although she is a good 2 hours away."

"My neighbors put out my trash bins. My daughter bought me a robotic vacuum cleaner and it's amazing."

"My friends and family help me I don't know what I would do without them."

"Friends (or lack of) don't really help me but my daughter has been a rock for me. When I was first signed off work back in October 2019 I had to apply for help from the government. 3 different forms to fill out 2 of which were like writing a novel. It was rediculous but we wanted to provide as much information as possible, we even used extra papers. She came to all my earlier hospital appointments, scans, etc…back in the beginning and recently started to come with me again. I would not have coped at the last one on my own and she's coming to my next scan in a few weeks as well as my Arterial Blood Gas Test. She helped me mentally as well, I already had therapy but I'm not sure I would be the way I am now if it hadn't been for my daughter. My daughter does all the shopping. Since the pandemic I don't like to go out much."

"My husband is my carer and does the cooking, cleaning, washing up, and hangs the washing for me. I am on Oxygen 24/7 but I have a cleaner comes in once a fortnight. He also does the shopping. I don't have much ironing but he does what is necessary. I would be lost without him. He gets a bit frustrated at times but I am pretty independent and try not to be too demanding."

"I suspect that every little bit helps. I'm still at a stage where I can do most things myself both inside the home and on the farm but really appreciate family/visitors just quietly pulling out the vacuum cleaner, going to the freezer to get something out for dinner and then cooking it. Once, in the supermarket park, a couple put the groceries in the car. They had noticed I was struggling. I would have got there by pacing myself but appreciated the thought of my fellow man."

"My family cooks many of my meals, carry things for me, help with washing, cleaning, and general household tasks. I have a home care package and my daughter is my carer. They shop for me, collect my prescriptions, drive me around if I can't drive on the day. My 4 adult children are all on the call list for my alarm. I am extremely fortunate."

"When having a picnic have it close to an handi-cap parking spot. My grandsons take out the trash. My Grand Daughter does most of the cooking. My son who I live with untangles my oxygen tube. My Great – Grand – Daughter – holds my O2 and calls me Great Grans Doggy. She is 3. My other Grand Daughter takes me to all my appointments. I could go on all day. I'm blessed."

"My wonderful children check on me daily, in person or by phone. My daughter drives about 140 km. on her day off to come and take me shopping with great patience, LOL. My grandson who is in mid - thirties goes out of his way to come and visit me almost every weekend. I am very proud and grateful."

"My neighbors bring my groceries in the house and have taken my Pug for walks while I'm having a difficult time breathing. My daughter – in – law picks me up whenever I need to go somewhere. I have a cleaning lady that comes in once a week. I try to do things myself, but appreciate all the help I get."

"My wife has done all the care taker work, plus everything else for the past 6 years."

"My husband does the hoovering, assists me with the changing, making bed. Assists me with cooking meals, washes my back and helps me shower. He carries my oxygen concentrator so it is easier for me to walk. Comes with me to all of my appointments. Puts away shopping when delivered. I would be absolutely lost without him."

"My daughter does all my shopping."

"My wife knows and tells me to stop trying to DIY. My daughters help me with shopping and lifting bags when we get back . Others ring to see how I'm doing etc…"

"My son and daughter live 300 miles away so don't expect them to, as for my hubby you would never know I had one."

"I cannot begin to tell you that's that my husband handles. He has been a blessing to me. Sometimes I will tell him please don't do anything else today. I need you around a long time. God is Good.!!!."

"My husband does the grocery shopping, laundry, and most of the cooking because he loves to cook. I have 2 housekeepers that come every 2 weeks. I also have 2 gardeners that come every 10 days. My husband is amazing and cooks 75% of the time."

"My husband does everything for me, I get breathless no matter what I do. At dinner time push myself to cook it goes really hard to breathe but I get it done, have bought an Air Physio it really works with bringing all the mucus up."

"My family or neighbor put out the bins. I strip the bed and my daughter puts clean sheets on, always a puffy job. Any heavy lifting they do and cleaning/gardening jobs I can't manage one or the other of my children help."

"I can manage most jobs but it does take some more time, sitting down and puffing in between. I'm very good at making up a list of jobs to be done, but some days I just look at it and think nah! There's always tomorrow."

"My youngest daughter is my carer. She has 3 children, 2 at school, last bub is turning 1. She does most things for me but Blue Carers' does cleaning each fortnight and on shop day every fortnight. Am grateful for any help."

"They slow down when walking with me, My wife takes my suitcases to the car on trips. When I play golf, nobody cares if I sit out a hole or two. Friends tend to speak in lower tones.

(that one I don't understand). My kids call more often. I'm more mellow. Small things don't bother me as much."

"My husband does all the cooking, our youngest son will come over after a bad snow storm to clear the driveway. Our oldest will come over and do carpentry work."

"I can do a lot myself. My husband vacuums, carries laundry baskets as I have back issues and A-fib, so he helps all he can. I do most all the cooking and cleaning otherwise. He always goes grocery shopping and carries the bags….He takes the trash out and the recycle to the dumpsters. He is my rock and very helpful and caring. My kids and grandkids don't realize what we do for each other, so not much help from them as they aren't around much and all have their own lives."

"My Son and Daughter help me with laundry and emptying trash. My son mows the yard and trims."

"My Son and his family help me so much. They do all the grocery shopping, running errands and taking out the trash.

My sister takes me to all of my tests at the hospital and my other appointments. My other Son lives 20 miles away and he checks on me every day. I still do dishes and laundry."

"Both my daughter, son and grandson are very helpful. If I need something all I have to do is ask especially if it is expensive they will have it for me every time. When my daughter is home she will cook for me. Grandson is here with me and if I need someone to drive me to an appointment he's always available. I try to be as independent as I can but they do what I need."

"My husband bought me a robotic vacuum and he does the laundry. My washer and dryer are in the basement so I would have to go up and down 2 large stairways."

"My hubby does everything as my breathing is too bad to do anything."

"Just that they are for me and I live with eldest daughter and son – in – law so I have no chores or cooking to do, I fold laundry and Swiffer that's it."

"My husband does some cooking, goes shopping for things that haven't been delivered, vacuums but doesn't dust. I pay my Niece to clean the house once a fortnight. She would have done it for nothing as she has a cleaning company though it was only fair to pay, and everything feels much cleaner. Other family lives in other parts of UK and although we are in touch rarely see each other."

"Steve 2936, my wife helps with my socks and shoes."

"I am able to do most things myself at the moment but my lively husband does the heavy work like gardening, vacuuming, and walking the dog (I have an ongoing hip problem). Even though he had a stroke 9 years ago but thank God he recovered fully."

"I have a cleaner who prepares my evening meal, husband is useless, hates sickness, he does the shopping, my grandchildren and daughter supply emotional support, take me out, do my hair, my female friends who I dance with just accept when I can't keep up and I am smothered in love by them, my family. I'm extremely lucky to have so much love around me. I am very thankful."

"My wife takes good care of me. She cooks vegan meals, does all the gardening and house work. I feel pretty useless sometimes, but I've learned that a lot of the things I used to do around the house I can't anymore. So when it's warm outside, I sometimes sit in the garden with her while she does the weeding and planting etc. I used to be concerned that the neighbors would think I was a slacker, but now I don't care what they think. Although my immediate neighbors know my condition I think understand my situation."

"My daughter helps me carry my backpack emergency oxygen tank for my nebulizer in it and makes me tea when I don't feel well. Everyone has been very kind and helpful to me. I'm lucky to have good support."

"I have a cleaner who comes in twice a week to do bathrooms, toilet, and floors. Family members all help out around the house. Changing bed linen when needed, shopping, cooking and washing. Assist me to appointments. I'm very lucky."

Chapter 7

Care varies all over the world we are finding. How do you feel your care is for your COPD? Good or bad and if so why?

"My care has been spotty for the past 2 years. When I first got diagnosed I had excellent care and saw my Pulmo. Doctor at least twice a year. I was in the hospital 5 times in the first 4 years with the disease flare-ups and he was in the hospital checking on me and was my primary care doctor when I was in the hospital. I almost died 3 times as I was very sick. His care was outstanding. Then I did not hear anything for a long time and got a call from a Pulmo. Doctor telling me that my doctor retired. He said that he wanted to see me. He was very nice and got me a PFT and when we got the results I was at 75% and it had been a drop from what it had been. He changed my prescription and said he would call me in 6 months and schedule another PFT. Well like he said, he called me and said that he would have his staff call me in 2 months to schedule another exam. Well, 8 months went by and I had not heard a thing. I called the office and found out he had retired and no one notified me. Well I was pissed. They had a new doctor call me a week later and he scheduled me for a PFT and the results came back that I was at 50%. I was floored and he gave me a new Inhaler and said he would see me in 4 months. Well, I had a situation I had to rectify a little later and found put that he had put in my records to not schedule me for 6 months. He had lied to me. I was ready to move to a new doctor association as a matter of fact had contacted another association. Well, in cussing out the admin. People I saw him 2 weeks later. He and I talked and he examined me and scheduled an appointment for 6 months from now and I believe he will keep this one or I will definitely move doctors."

"Hello Steve hope your keeping well. I have received excellent care from my (new) Dr. and my Consultant who is one of the top lung Consultants in the country at Kings College Hospital, London. I could not wish for better. The support care and empathy I believe is phenomenal."

"My care was not good IMO in the beginning. Pulmonologist simply told me I had emphysema and prescribed Anoro Ellipta. Had rash and face swelling a week after on this med. Called his office for advice because this could have been a reaction according to the literature. Never got a call back so I went to the ER. I felt I was treated this way because at the time I was still smoking but reducing but was on Chantix. My treatment improved when my GP got involved and ordered another CT scan and a Pulm. Function Test. Within a week I got a call from the Pulmo. Office giving me an appointment which is for today. As I am now 4 months smoke free perhaps his attitude will be more attentive. By the way, he is not a bad guy. I have more confidence on my care as I have an excellent GP. She will talk on the phone once a month."

"Terrible I have not seen anybody in 2 years they just do not care."

"I haven't had an X-ray in over a year."

"Haven't seen a GP for 2 ½ years but my respiratory nurses are brilliant. See them at least twice a year and they also phone to check up. Have no problems with getting medications from GP, so I'm happy the way it is at present."

"Very bad, I have not seen anyone since coming out of the hospital."

"I have not seen a respiratory nurse or GP about my COPD for 3 years and due a telephone call from nurse next week. How can she tell possibly from that if I am on the right medications etc…"

"Hi, I also haven't seen a GP or nurse for about 3 years."

"Well Steve, my care is quite good."

"Hi Steve, I had COPD 15 years. I live in Ireland & only see GP….every few months….He does spirometry test and prescribes inhaler. I do want to change my doc. but here they are not taking on new patients since covid started."

"I have received more information and help from this site than my GP, who will only treat me for asthma, but symptoms for COPD my treatment has been very poor."

"I live in the USA and see my general doctor once a year for med. refills but I can see him if I have an exacerbation in between or just sick in general! I'm satisfied and try to stay healthy.!"

"I'm in the USA and my Dr. is ok. He does talk a bit about how I am doing but not enough. I have sleep apnea as well and he doesn't say much if anything about it."

"I had to request the Trelegy that I take now, my doctor did not suggest it and I feel better now."

"My care is pretty much non - existent. Supposed to have a check up with a nurse (never a doctor) every two years. Not had one for about four years. If I ask, I get reply" can't do it now, covid "Could do with an inhaler but pretty much given up now."

"They seem to be using covid as an excuse for everything nowadays. I only see a practice nurse too and on list for consultant but still waiting."

"Hi Steve. I feel my care is fantastic. My GP and my lung specialist know each other, work in the same private clinic (lung doctor also works at a hospital) and they talk to each other as all the time. They both ring me up to make sure I'm going along OK. I am so lucky."

"Well I saw my pulmonologist yesterday. My stats are good at 85% lung function and 96 PO. The thing is I had to remind him of the second scap PET before I found out. He seemed a bit peeved that the GP that took the lead and ordered these tests and asked if I would be mad at him if the next follow up is in a year. He feels that GP is a little over cautious."

"Feel it is up to me to manage it. I was meant to see the pulmonary consultant a few months ago and even though my condition is getting worse his secretary rang and said I could not have an in person appointment at the hospital so it was a phone call instead."

"I'm in Australia and we receive wonderful care. I only see my GP, but I've been with him 40 years as our family Dr. I see him once a month and I can phone anytime I need. He always makes sure I've got repeat scripts and anti-biotics at home in case."

"I went for my repeat prescription today only to find the pharmacy didn't order my inhaler!. As the doctor's were open I had a word with the receptionist who assured me she would have words with the GP and get a prescription sorted. Fast forwards to 17:45, the surgery and the chemist closed at 18:00, I rang the doctors and spoke to the receptionist who said…

and I quote "do you need it? I didn't think it was urgent and it won't be looked at until Monday Morning."

"My pharmacy are always telling me sorry it's not on the system I say well ring up my GP because he assures he has sent it and I'm not leaving here without it. You got rights and they just haven't been bothered most times tell them to ring your Gp while you wait you will they soon find it on their system then. LOL!."

"Hi, I must be very lucky, I have a doctor GP and also my Lung Specialist I can talk to on the phone, my doctor gives any prescriptions I need to Pharmacy in same building and they deliver within a couple of days free of charge. I am in Australia, New South Wales Sydney, South Western Suburbs."

"I certainly find that some pharmacists and GP software does not seem to match…from recent general experience in my village….I feel human communication has been lost somewhat."

"Yes, my pulmonary doctor has no time to see me. Tells me she'll call me when she wants to see me. That was 8 months ago. I since had to find a new doctor who is up on her toes with tests, new prescriptions, and keeping me informed on results."

"At the present I don't have a pulmonary doctor."

"I don't have a pulmonologist either. I don't really need one at this stage. I had one in the beginning to help get the ball rolling, as they say, but now my PCP handles prescribing my meds and we discuss if it's time to try something different. This PCP can also order up tests if/when necessary."

"It is the same everywhere and it's exhausting I know. We have to be in charge of our medical care 100%. from keeping copies of all our blood work, tests and procedures results to calling daily to get our proper medicines in a timely manner. We are just a number in most cases."

"My Pulmonologist is excellent he is always very supportive and gives me samples of any new drug he thinks might help. That is how I found out about Breztri and it made a significant difference in my breathing. If your pulmonologist is not supportive find a new one."

"Yes, I am lucky with my Lung Specialist as well, he will try any new products he thinks might help me, if they don't we just go back to the old one. I am able to call him any time and he gets back to me when it is convenient, the same with my GP, so pleased I have to have great doctors that is why I didn't change when we moved."

"The hoops we need to jump is insane. I had an insurance change, and am still fighting to get my meds approved & filled since the New Year started. Pharmacy says call the doctor and doctor says call the insurance, insurance says call the pharmacy it is a vicious circle and who suffers? me of course."

"Yes, I had loads of trouble with my doctor. When you phone your doctor ask for the practice manager tell him or her your problem and they will sort it out."

"Better to e- mail them, then you have proof and they can't say you didn't get in touch. That way you just keep replying to the same e-mail and you have a paper trail."

"I'm so glad I enjoy a good system here in Ontario (Canada). My stuff is ready at the pharmacy by the time I get there from my doctor. About 20 minutes."

"Hi, my health care is under my GP. I have never been referred to a Pulmonologist."

"My Lung doctor resigned. No notice and no replacement."

"I see my lung specialist every 6 months and my oncologist every 6 months on the in between times so they both keep each other informed as well as forwarding copies of all visits, scans etc. to my GP. My GP sees me every fortnight to check everything. I get the very best of care and I'm grateful."

"Hi, I am in Australia. My GP will fax prescriptions to pharmacy who will deliver….once a month is free, other deliveries cost about 5 dollars. My GP had given me her mobile number if I am in dire straits, or I can ring the surgery and ask for her to ring me. I can also make phone appointments with the GP and my Lung Specialist."

"After reading all these problems I feel so lucky, I am in Sydney Australia. I have a GP who will always ring me back when it is convenient and my Lung Specialist I speak to every 3 months unless I have a problem and then I can ring and get him to contact when he can."

"I haven't seen my Pulm. Dr. in 4 or 5 years. It was always the PA or MA. Just 2 weeks ago I found out my Pulm. Dr. left some time ago. Do you think they could have informed me? I have an appt. Tuesday and they are definitely going to hear how happy I am about it."

"My Pulm. prescribed Anoro for COPD. I inhaled the first dose and it made me so dizzy, I hit the deck and am bruised and sore. I called the office to see if they wanted to change the Rx. No response. Called again, after a couple of days, still no response. Pharmacist told me to stop using it. He finally got an answer and they switched me to Spriva. This was way back in January. Get to know your Pharmacist, great resource."

"Hi Steve, I have received excellent care right across the board. I live in Guilford but my main treatment is at Guy's and St. Thomas's in London for both my lungs and chronic leg pain caused by a nerve tumor. I can be seen at either of the hospitals in London but always the same doctors as all work at both together as it is the same trust. I was actually in St. Thomas's after a 2nd. Operation on my leg which was supposed to be an overnight stay but ended up 2 weeks. Chest X-rays, CT scan, lung function and MRI countless ABG's and 3 or 4 blood taken. Sent home diagnosed with severe COPD, Emphysema, Pulmonary Hypertension and a lung disease called Neurofibromatosis related to lung disease which causes fibrosis and cysts in the lungs and 3 liters of Oxygen. I've since been back to London quite a few times but only twice to the chest clinic. I'm monitored by local respiratory teams at the hospital in Guilford and are only a phone call away and are out within 48 hours if I need to see them. My own GP is excellent, he listens and explains things as clearly as do my doctors but I believe in asking lots of questions as well and I have good knowledge of what is happening to me and my condition. My care while I was in the hospital for those 2 weeks at St. Thomas was second to none and the nurses were amazing. I also have a carer that comes in every morning that helps me get washed or bathed and dressed and changes my bed, hoovers, empties my bins and other light housework who I would be lost without. I feel completely comfortable with him, patient caring nature as well as empathy and respect."

"I haven't seen a GP for 2 ½ years but my Respiratory Nurses are brilliant. See them at least twice a year and they also phone to check up on me. Have no problems with getting medications from GP. So I'm quite happy the way it is at the moment. The surgery has just sent me an on-line questionaire re…My COPD at the moment !!!. Mind you my surgery has failed it's oqc and is in extreme measures!!! Which means they have 6 months to sort or another administration team will be sent in!!!. Shame as nurses I have are so good!!!."

"Pretty bad, I've not seen a doc or nurse for 3 years. When I see others on here with specialist lung doctors I am envious. My breathing is getting worse and seeing a doc is almost impossible."

"Just to see the Respiratory Nurse at the doctor's office every 6 months to a year unless I make an appointment to see the doctor. Last year I really felt poorly about this time and went to see the doctor to ask if there was anything they could do to help my breathing. Doc said "Your getting all the help you can have. All the inhalers are the same so no point changing them no good having a nebulizer yet, go and see the nurse next week". Luckily she told me to take Carbostecine and that helped but that's it. I feel abandoned and down most of the time."

"Hi Steve, I have had COPD for `15 years. I live in Ireland and only see GP every few months. He does Spirometry test and prescribes inhaler. I do want to change my doc. But here they are not taking new patients due to covid."

"Good evening everybody. I have been reading the comments on this question. I am amazed at some of you not seeing anybody for months sometimes for years. I see my Pulm. Doctor every 4 months and my GP every 6 months. Also through MY CHART, I can ask for refills on prescriptions. Ask questions all most always get an answer in 12 hours. I have learned a long time ago you have to ask your doctor questions if you need answers about your health."

"In my case once a year is not enough and the doctors don't have the answers."

"I live in the USA and see my general doctor once a year for med. refills but I can see him if I have a exacerbation in between or just sick in general!! I'm satisfied and try to stay healthy!!"

"I had to request Trelegy that I take now, my doctor didn't suggest it and I feel better."

"My care is not good, only person I see when needed is the practice nurse and I've stopped smoking 5 years ago and have lost weight and go to the gym and try to help myself but cannot get to see the consultant, the wait is 5 years and I'm waiting 3 years and it will probably be worse now after covid."

"Hi Steve, I live in Australia and have wonderful care from my doctor (anytime I want), lung specialist every 6 months and Oncologist every 3 months. Support group at hospital every month and nurses to ask questions of any time."

"My care is pretty much non-existant. I'm Supposed to have a check-up with a nurse (never a doctor) every 2 years. Not had one for about 4 years. If I ask, get reply" can't do it now covid "Could do with an inhaler but pretty much have given up."

"My care is wonderful, I go between the VA (…..authors note…Veterans Administration in America) hospital in

Madison, Wisconsin and the VA clinic in Rockford, Illinois, I also go to Pulmonary Rehab. At St. Margaret's Hospital in Peru, Illinois. Pretty much anything I want or need is handled in a timely manner. My doctor's work together by phone or FAX to be sure there are no overlaps and my meds. are correct. With my lung, heart and physical problems I do not think I could get a better health care system in the world, thanks to the US Army.

"When I was first diagnosed the care was very good. However three years ago we moved to a small town with limited resources. We moved because I wanted to move out of our townhouse because there were to many people who smoked around us, which I couldn't control, and to buy a detached house was too expensive in the big city. Now we have a small rancher and the neighbors don't smoke. The trade-off which I knew would be there is that medical care in a small town is not as available as in the city. We have a new family doctor, but basically feel I'm on my own."

Chapter 8

My Friends and Family Can help Me Best By:

"Giving their opinions."

"Supporting me emotionally & giving me a hand sometimes when I need it."

"Being there for me."

"My friends and family can help me best by understanding my condition and my limitations, let me do things in my own time and not to rush me."

"Steve, all the comments made by our friends said it all. Thanks for writing this book. Looking forward to reading it."

"Accepting me unconditionally I am."

"Trying to understand better what it is like to have to force yourself to function most days. The want and need to do things is there but not always the ability."

"Not thinking I am trying to get out of doing things, like cleaning my house, shopping, etc. just because I have COPD."

"Understanding my condition."

"Helping me to breathe properly and to keep me calm."

"Understanding my limitations."

"Listening to me as I explain what is going on with me. Have understanding with compassion in helping me deal with it daily."

"Showing support and understanding that I may not do things as fast as I did, but I can still do them."

"By understanding that each day is different for me and when I plan to do something, it may not happen."

"Be patient and understanding. Don't hold it against me when I can't be somewhere or do something. Be considerate. And check on me, even if it is a text."

"when I can, at my own pace as I need to try and live a normal life."

"Understanding this disease was not my choice, never smoked or drank alcohol but here I am. Not the mum or wife I used to be but still the same person that loves them. Patience to understand that even though I try it is much slower that before. To know that I do the best I can."

"My friends and family can help me by listening and being there when I need them."

"Accepting my condition."

"Patience and Understanding."

"By loving me unconditionally."

"Helping out more in the home, for example, shopping and housework."

"Just supporting me and my decisions."

"My family and friends can help me best by encouraging me to get out more, but also understanding how this awful disease has destroyed my confidence and limits to do the things I want to do."

"Keeping me mentally and physically active."

"Praying."

"Understanding my limitations."

"Understanding I have a chronic disease and will probably get worse."

"My friends and family can help me best by understanding that I am limited to what I can do now."

"Believing me. And by the way Steve: congratulations on finishing the book."

"Themselves."

"Accepting me as I am - with my growing list of recently acquired limitations."

"Learning about the disease."

'By being more available to listen to your situation and do research to help and understand when you are going through."

"Learning my about my condition, and understanding the sometime Herculean effort that it takes for me to participate in family functions."

"I live alone with my dog..but I know I have to get up moving to keep my airways open and mucus loose with lots of water…"

"No Judging."

"By being optimistic for me."

"My friends and family can help me best by helping me change my bed and bringing in the groceries from the car."

"My friends and family can help me the best by having compassion and understanding my limitations."

"My friends and family can help me the best by trying to understand that when I say no to doing something I am struggling more than they would ever understand and to take my no as a no and get I am not super woman!."

"Just understanding."

"My friends and family can help me the best by getting vaxxed."

"Trying to understand why we can do so little in such a long time."

"Believing when I say I'm not feeling well and need an ambulance.

Not saying "You have not taken all your meds. Have you done all this or that. When the answer is yes."

That's the time the paramedics could be looking after you and getting you where you need to be."

Authors note…..anyone who does not call an ambulance in these cases should be up on charges for abuse.

"I go to a COPD maintenance class and the guy that takes it did a course and part of the course was walking up and down a room then they put a straw in your mouth and told to breathe through it and see how far they could go as this like having COPD so tell them to breathe through a straw and see how far they could go and get a little taste of your life."

"Understanding how debilitating this disease is and help at some of the household chores that I really struggle to do. Changing beds, cleaning baths etc…"

"Being there when I need them and understanding that I have limitations. I do try to so as much as I can on my own but some things are hard such as yard work and heavy cleaning. I try not to use my health as a crutch."

"My friends and family can help me best by truly understanding my limitations, by being patient and thoughtful."

"I'm lucky, I have family, friends and a doctor who give me the support I need without impinging on my freedom. Not everybody has this by and means. My friends and my family can help me best by…..listening while I explain just what COPD and Emphysema are, what the physical downsides are, that some days are better than others. I have a CD of my lungs from which I printed off some shots - this is for two reasons - what I am dealing with and why they shouldn't!!! smoke, vape or do anything else silly that involves their lungs.

I suspect that sadly, even when it is explained to them, that many people, including family members, either don't care or can't assimilate the problem leaving people feeling isolated or alone.

Good luck with the book Steve for the reasons we've probably all just mentioned."

"Actually understanding how serious my condition actually is. Living on my own and having my daughter for support, a brother who never listens when I'm explaining things, worries all the time about me but rarely visits. Having patience as well."

"Being supportive and understanding that may help, because when I can't breathe I am not making the best decisions without even knowing, don't use my disease to take your advantage of me."

"My friends and family can help me best by truly understanding my limitations, by being patient and thoughtful."

"My friends and family by being supportive and understanding my limitations."

"Helping me when I ask but let me do what I can when I can, at my own pace as I need to try and live a normal life."

"…..help me the best by being patient, give me the time to do things at my pace and don't try and chivvy me along thinking that helps!!!."

"Understanding my limitations. When they understand then I know they won't push me to go beyond those limits. Then I feel safe and I am more likely to enjoy myself no matter what we are doing."

"My friends and family can help me by giving me emotional and practical support when needed."

"Helping me to breathe properly and help me to keep calm"

"Having compassion for my predicament and listening to what I need especially what I don't need, eg: not using perfumes and scents around me. By not getting frustrated at my limitations."

Steve 2936, "For being there for me. Take care."

"Giving me space when I am struggling. Understand that I can't help as much as I did."

"My family and friends could help me by learning more about COPD, Emphysema, Pulmonary Hypertension and Heart Failure. I am a widow at 81 and it's just me and my dog Stella. My family does not understand the seriousness of these diseases. I wish they would look at the website or Google info. so they would realize the challenges that we face. My children help take me to the doctor visits and come whenever I ask for help but I sense they don't think I am as sick as I am. I don't want sympathy as I try to do as much as I can but there are some things that I just cannot do. My 02 drops into the 70's with just a little exertion. Good Luck with the book."

Made in the USA
Monee, IL
23 June 2022

98370218R00069